Creating
Christmas
Ornaments

from Polymer Clay

10 Original Designs with
Step-by-Step Instructions

Bridget
C.
Albano

Text written with and photography by Jeffrey B. Snyder

Schiffer Publishing Ltd

77 Lower Valley Road, Atglen, PA 19310

CONTENTS

DEDICATION

THIS BOOK IS DEDICATED TO DANNY AND DANA, THE DELIGHT OF MY HEART.

Book Design by (M_J) Hannigan

Published by Schiffer Publishing Ltd.
77 Lower Valley Road
Atglen, PA 19310
Please write for a free catalog.
This book may be purchased from the publisher.
Please include $2.95 postage.
Try your bookstore first.

We are interested in hearing from authors
with book ideas on related topics.

Library of Congress Cataloging-in-Publication Data

Albano, Bridget C.
   Creating Christmas ornaments from polymer clay :
10 original designs with step-by-step instructions /
Bridget C. Albano ; text written with and photography by Jeffrey B. Snyder.
    p. cm.
   ISBN 0-88740-850-8 (paper)
   1. Plastics craft. 2. Christmas decorations. I.
Snyder , Jeffrey B. II. Title.
TT297.A53   1995
745.594' 12--dc20   95-14948
                             CIP

INTRODUCTION
& HELPFUL HINTS

Polymer clay is one of the most versatile arts and crafts materials ever invented. It is relatively soft, easy to form, and will not harden until you bake it. (I once started a project and couldn't decide how to finish it. I covered this work-in-progress with plastic wrap to keep out the dust and put it away. Six months later I pulled the project out again, finished it, and finally baked it.) Once baked, polymer clays are hard, durable, waterproof, and their colors will not fade.

I use four different kinds of polymer clay — Fimo, Cernit, Sculpey, and Pro Mat. All four have their advantages for different projects and you will soon have your own favorites. They come in an array of beautiful colors (many with a metallic or pearlescent sparkle) so your projects don't have to be painted once they are baked. Sculpey is the softest, and therefore usually recommended for children's use. (Children don't have the hand strength necessary for kneading the other clays, nor the patience to do so.) Sculpey is a favorite with adults as well ... who also have little patience for kneading. If you want the finished product to be a little more durable, mix Pro Mat with the Sculpey (or Cernit or Fimo — they all mix together nicely). Fresh packages of Cernit, Fimo, and Pro Mat are not too hard to knead — it's the older packages that give us trouble. Adding a drop or two of baby oil or mineral oil will help soften up clay that has become too hard or crumbly. Rubbing your hands with hand cream or vaseline before kneading also works. And there is a soft, clay-like additive called Mix Quick that works even better.

Baking your projects on glass assures even heat distribution. I use glass sheets from old 5" x 7" and 8" x 10" picture frames. Glass baking pans are excellent but it is not recommended that you cook food on pans that have been used for polymer clay baking. Baking on metal pans or aluminum foil is tricky — pieces seem to burn more easily, so check them often. You will know when you have over-baked something — the colors will be darker and muddy, and the edges may brown.

That brings us to correct baking procedures. Most home ovens are fine, including toaster ovens and convection ovens (don't use microwave ovens). As for time and temperature, all of the polymer clay artists I know have different combinations that work best for them. My favorite is to bake almost everything at 265 degrees for 30 to 35 minutes in a toaster oven that has not been preheated. Thick objects require longer baking times at slightly lowered tem-

peratures. On my toaster oven (an old Sears model), only the bottom heating element heats up when it is on "Bake"; I use the top oven rack (as far as possible from the heat), located in about the center of the oven. In my home kitchen oven, both the top and bottom elements heat up on "Bake", but on the center rack the clay bakes fine. The most important thing is to make sure your oven's temperature is **accurate**. Purchase an oven thermometer. Mine was less than $3.00 at the grocery store. There is often a big difference between the temperature you select and the temperature in the oven. My toaster oven has to be set on 312 degrees in order to reach 265 degrees.

Baking pieces on glass will create shiny spots on the back of the clay where it rests on the glass. This isn't a problem unless you are baking something that needs to look good on all sides — such as a bead or a dangle earring. Bake these pieces on an ordinary slip of paper on top of the glass and you will eliminate shiny spots.

Your hands will need cleaning often. The best cleaner I've tried is Boraxo powdered hand soap. For lighter cleaning at your work area, baby wipes are convenient.

Allow baked pieces to cool thoroughly before handling; warm pieces break easily. Once cool, pop them off the baking surface by loosening all the sides first. Be careful not to break off arms and legs. However, if something does break, Super Glue Gel is an excellent and permanent remedy. Remember that pieces can be baked again as often as necessary, even with glued parts.

Repairs are relatively easy for polymer clay projects. For example, if half of the wing of an angel ornament breaks off and is lost, first remove the hanging ribbon, then trim the rest of the wing off with wire cutters or an X-acto knife. (You could repair the broken part of the wing, but the joint would not be as strong and it wouldn't look the same as the other wing.) Make a new wing and apply it to the body as you did the original wing. Bake the repaired ornament for the same amount of time and at the same temperature as the original baking. Note that if the wing broke because it was under-baked, you will need to increase either your baking time or temperature.

These designs are presented for your personal use and enjoyment. They are not for commercial reproduction by employees or for sale through commercial outlets. I hope you enjoy creating beautiful clay art as much as I do.

SOURCES FOR SUPPLIES

Most large craft shops and art supply stores carry Fimo and Sculpey, and sometimes Cernit or Pro Mat. Occasionally, these products are found near the doll houses since many miniatures enthusiasts use polymer clay to make tiny fruits and vegetables. The same craft shops will also carry most of the other supplies you will need.

An excellent mail order source is:
The Clay Factory of Escondido
P.O. Box 460598
Escondido, CA 92046-0598
1-800-243-3466

The Clay Factory sells Fimo, Cernit, Pro Mat, and jewelry findings to retail or wholesale customers. They also sell interesting pattern cutters including animal shapes, hearts, and flowers.

If you'd like to get your local craft shop to carry Sculpey or Pro Mat, ask them to contact:
Polyform Products Co.
P.O. Box 2119
Schiller Park, IL 60176
Sales ofc. (708) 678-4836

Or your shop can contact The Clay Factory of Escondido as a wholesale customer to order Fimo, Cernit, or Pro Mat.

The wooden beads that I use come from Christmas tree garlands.

Here are the polymer clays readily available in the United States. Left to right: Sculpey III, Pro Mat — both from Polyform Products, Cernit, and FIMO - both from Germany.

There is more than one way to flatten the clay. On the left is a brayer and on the right is a pasta machine with 7 different settings for different thicknesses. You may also use a rolling pin or even a dowel. (Don't use those pasta machines or rolling pins for food after they have flattened clay.)

You will need these tools — or similar items — to work the clay: two different X-acto knife blades, a tissue slicing blade, a ceramics tool, two leather working tools, toothpicks, and a hat pin. These particular items work best for me.

Needle-nose pliers, wire cutters, round-nose pliers and twenty gauge brass wire will also be used to create wire loops.

Sculpting Christmas Ornaments
Twig Reindeer With Heart

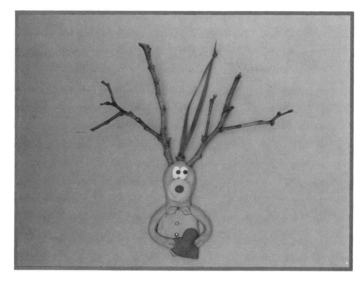

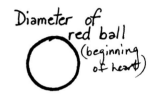

Diameter of red ball (beginning of heart)

This is the Twig Reindeer with Hearts. The materials used were Sculpey Bronze, Sculpey White, Sculpey Black, Cernit Doll Flesh, Cernit Red, Pro Mat Green Pearl, one red seed bead, two 3 mm brass beads, red ribbon for hanging, 24 gauge wire for a hanging loop, and one set of antler twigs.

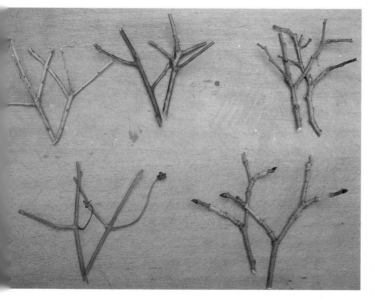

Always cut twigs green. To check if the twigs are green, bend the branches a bit. If they bend, the twigs should be fine. If they break, discard them. Remember, the heat from baking will dry the twigs. The twigs here are (left to right, top to bottom) wild persimmon, oak, locust, wild grape vine and sycamore.

Using an X-acto knife, whittle the ends of the twigs so they will slide easily into the clay.

Make a loop for hanging the ornament out of 24 gauge wire. Wrap the wire around the thick part of your needle-nose pliers, twist a couple times, and snip off the finished loop with wire cutters.

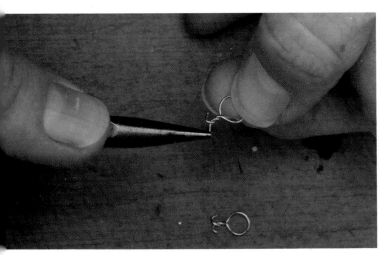

Turn up the ends with long-nose pliers as shown. This will prevent loops from slipping out after baking.

Take a 2 ounce block of Sculpey Bronze and cut it into four equal pieces. Each 1/2 ounce piece will make one reindeer.

Cut off about 1/5 of this block and save it for later.

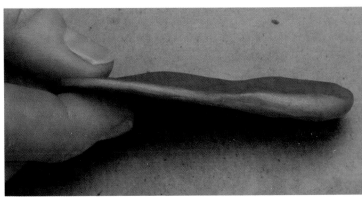

Begin kneading the rest of the block and shape into the reindeer body. Keep the head about twice as thick as the rest of the body, especially the upper part where the antlers go. Let the head thickness taper down through the neck so that the neck is a bit thicker than the rest of the body.

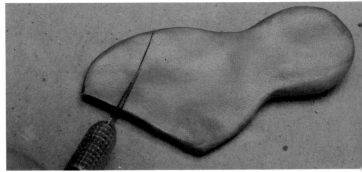

Hold the piece up to the pattern to check the size, then cut the bottom of the body into a V shape.

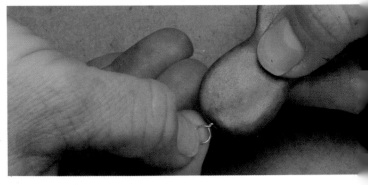

Insert the hanging loop into the top of the head now, pressing firmly.

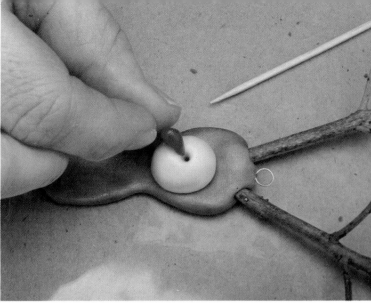

Insert the antlers - one on each side of the loop. Place the reindeer on your baking glass.

Make a hole in the center of the muzzle with a toothpick. Insert the pointed end of the nose into the hole. Press firmly into place.

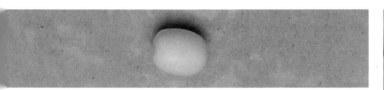

Clean your hands well, then knead a small piece of Cernit Doll Flesh. Roll between your palms to form a ball about the size of a marble. Elongate it slightly into a cylinder.

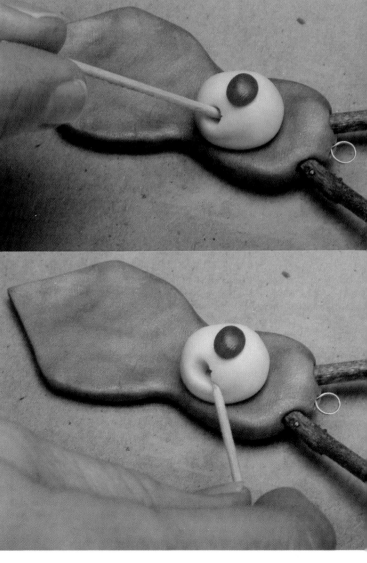

Press the cylinder firmly into the reindeer's face.

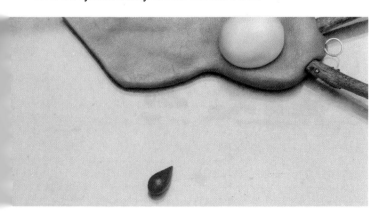

Make a teardrop shaped nose out of Cernit Red.

To make the mouth, create a small hole on the side of the muzzle with your toothpick. Gently press upward with the tip of the toothpick to make a smile.

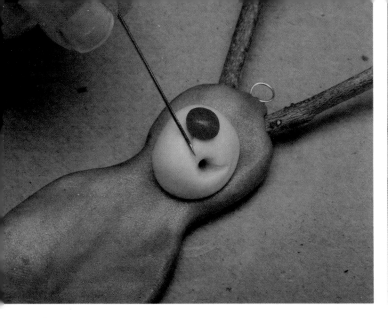

Make a line from the nose to the mouth with a hat pin or knife.

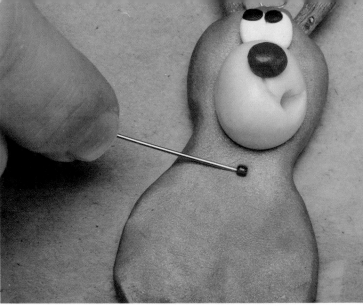

With a hat pin or similar item, pick up a red seed bead and place it in the center of the reindeer's neck. Press firmly.

Roll two small ovals of Sculpey White for eyes. Press onto the face.

Roll a small roll of Pro Mat Green Pearl. Flatten it and cut diagonally across the roll to make two leaves.

Firmly press on two small black clay dots to complete the eyes.

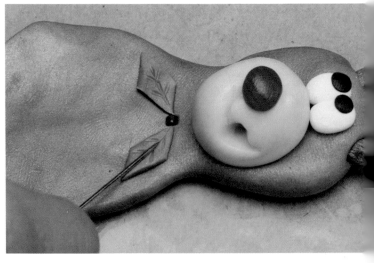

Place the two leaves on either side of the bead. Press into place. Draw on leaf lines with the hat pin.

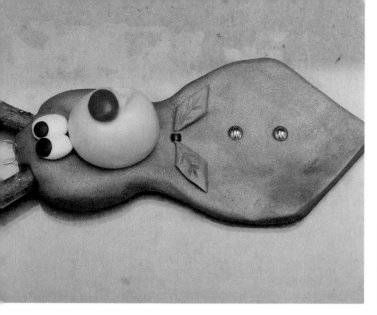

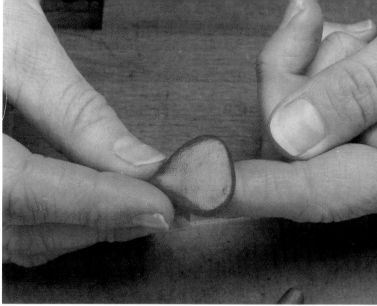

With a toothpick lift each brass bead into place. When in position, press firmly into the clay body.

Form a small ball of red clay (see pattern for size), flatten it with your finger tips, and pull one end into a point.

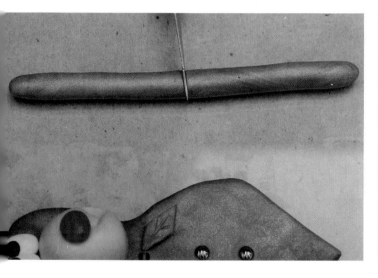

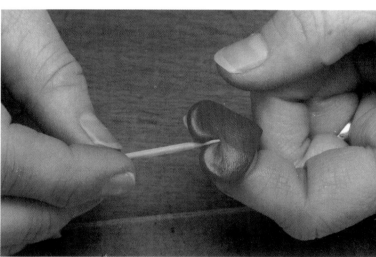

Now take the 1/5 piece of Bronze clay you cut off in the beginning of this project and roll it into a 3 1/4" long roll. Cut the roll in half to form two arms.

With your finger nail, knife, or toothpick, gently press into the rounded end to make a heart shape.

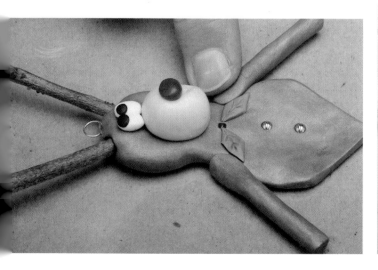

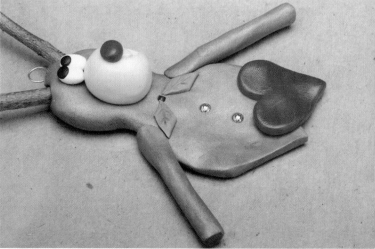

Press just the shoulders onto the body next to the green leaves. Press firmly so they won't come off after baking.

When the heart is shaped, press it firmly onto the bottom of the reindeer's body as shown.

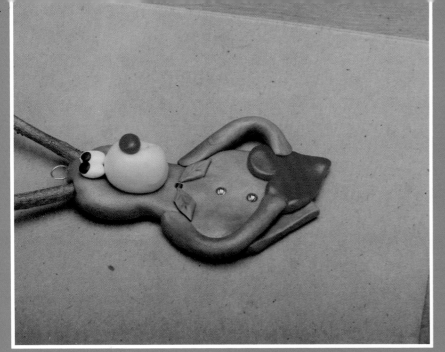

Bend arms to touch the heart and press them in place firmly.

Make hoof indentations with a toothpick.

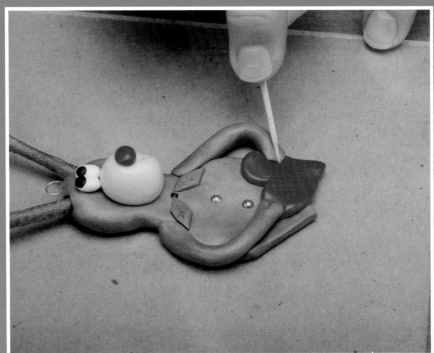

Your reindeer is now ready to bake at 265 degrees for 34 minutes. When he has baked and thoroughly cooled, gently pop him off the baking sheet. Check for antler looseness. If they slide out of the hole, put in a drop of glue and carefully slide them back in place. Cut a 9 1/2" length of 1/8" wide satin ribbon for hanging. Tie a knot in the end and thread it through the hanging loop as shown.

TWIG ANTLERED, FULL-BODY REINDEER

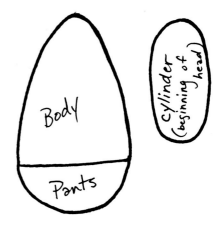

This is the Twig Antlered, Full-body Reindeer. The materials used here are Sculpey Bronze, Scupley White, Sculpey Green Brilliant, Cernit Red, Pro Mat Green Pearl, red or green seed beads, two black seed beads, 24 gauge wire for a hanging loop, one set of twig antlers, red ribbon for hanging, and a pre-baked candy cane.

Roll it between your palms with even pressure, making the roll longer and thinner as you roll.

When you are satisfied with the roll's thinness, cut and shape it into candy canes. Bake on a slip of paper on top of your glass baking sheet to prevent shiny spots. Bake at 265 degrees for about 20 minutes.

This little roll will make about 5 candy canes. Roll a small core of Sculpey White, about an inch long, and wrap a flattened strip of Cernit Red around it, twisting as you wrap. Wrap a thinner strip of Sculpey Green Brilliant between the red stripes.

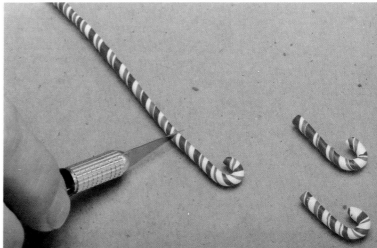

The first steps in creating this reindeer are the same as those performed in the first project except for your choice of antlers, which should be a little bit smaller. Make a wire hanging loop, then cut the Sculpey Bronze block into 4 equal pieces as shown in the previous project. Take one of these 1/4 blocks and cut it into three equal pieces.

Roll one of these three pieces into a cylinder matching the size of the pattern. This will be the head.

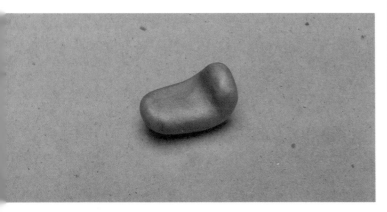

Flatten it slightly, turning one end up into a muzzle as shown.

Take another third and shape it by hand into the body. Cut off the excess clay and save it. You may also flatten the clay to about 2 mm thick, lay the pattern on top and cut out the body with a knife.

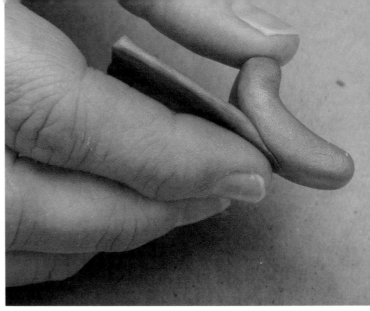

Attach the pointed end of body to the back of the head by pressing them together firmly.

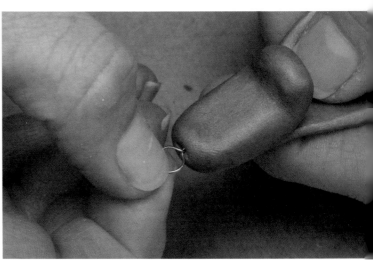

Insert the hanging loop into the top of the head now and press in well.

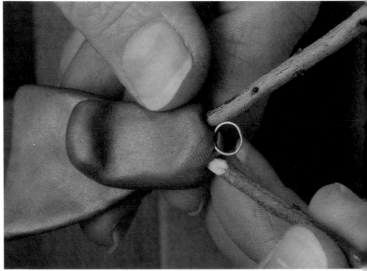

Insert the antlers, one on each side of the hanging loop. Press them into the clay firmly. Place the reindeer on a baking glass.

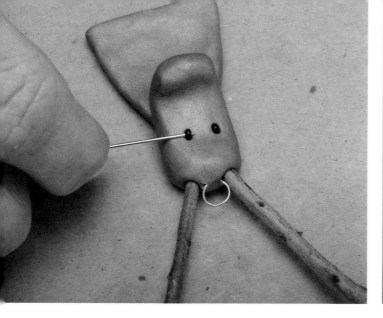

Pick up black seed beads with a hat pin and press them into the head for eyes.

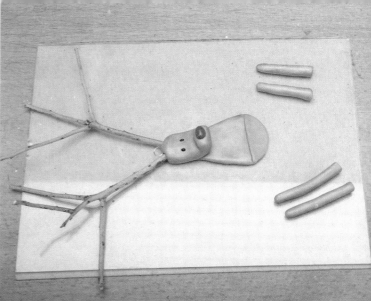

Knead together the remaining pieces of bronze clay. Roll into a long, thin roll 6 1/2" long. Cut two pieces 1 3/4" long each for arms. Cut two pieces 1 1/2" long for legs.

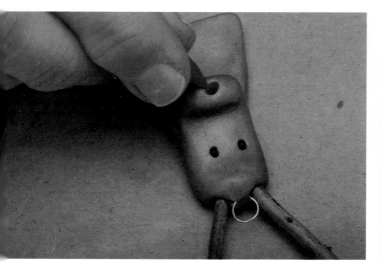

Roll a small amount of red clay into a teardrop shape for the nose. Make a hole in the up-turned muzzle with a toothpick and insert the nose, pointed end down. Press in well.

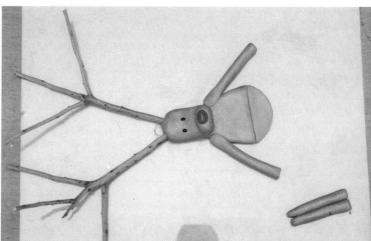

Lightly press the two legs together. Attach the arms to the body by firmly pressing down at the shoulders.

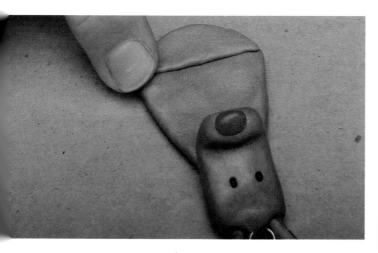

Flatten out a piece of Pro Mat Green Pearl. Cut out a piece to fit the pants pattern. Press firmly onto the body of the reindeer, overlapping slightly.

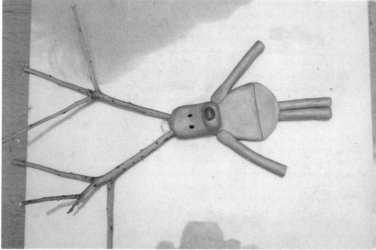

Lift up the bottom of the pants, slide in the legs about 1/4", and then firmly press the pants back down.

13

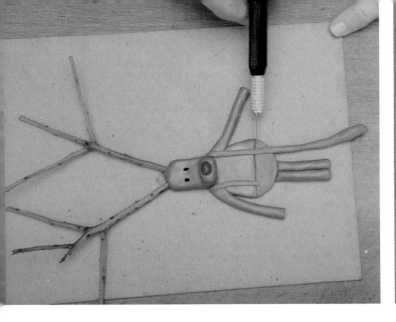

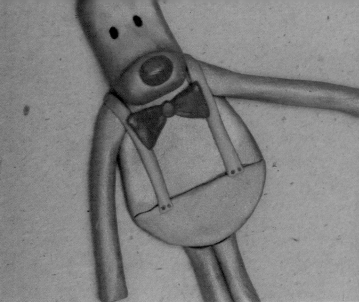

Roll a long, thin roll of Pro Mat Green Pearl for suspenders. Flatten slightly. Lay the roll along the suspender line and cut it off when it overlaps the pants. Press down lightly.

With a toothpick, make indentations for folds of the bow tie. Press a small dot of red clay into the center of the bow.

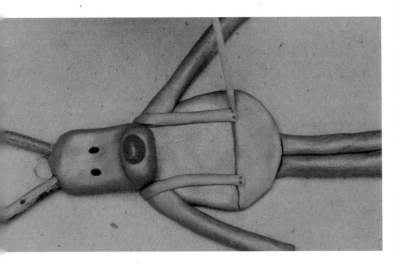

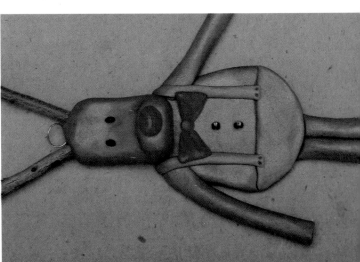

Make "buttons" with the tip of a toothpick.

Press in two red or green seed beads on the body for buttons.

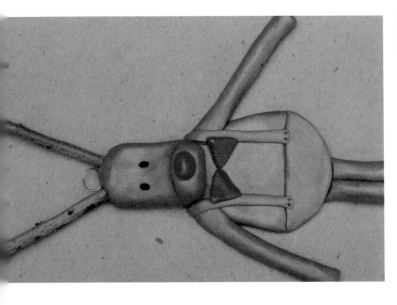

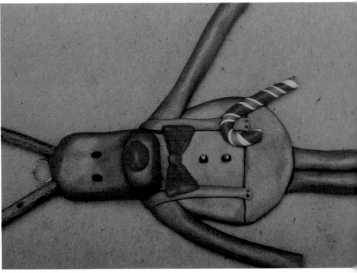

Form two small triangles out of Cernit Red and press into place at the neck.

Lightly press down the pre-baked candy cane in the position indicated in the picture.

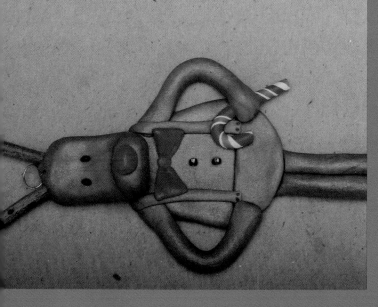 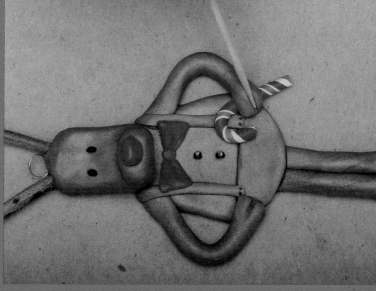

Bend the reindeer's arms and press them firmly onto the body and the candy cane.

Make hoof marks with a toothpick.

Bake at 265 degrees for 34 minutes. When baked and thoroughly cooled, gently pop your reindeer off the baking sheet. Check for loose antlers. If they slide out of the holes, put in a drop of glue and carefully slide them back into place. Attach a red hanging ribbon as shown previously.

SNOWMAN

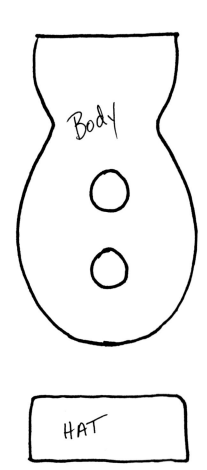

Snowman Twig ornament. Materials: Sculpey White, Sculpey Rose, Sculpey Pink Pearl, Cernit Black, Cernit Red, Pro Mat Green Pearl, two black seed beads, one set of twigs for arms, a wire hanging loop, ribbon for hanging, ribbon for scarf, one red seed bead, and hot glue.

Cut twigs for the snowman's arms. See the section on the reindeer twigs. You do not have to whittle the ends for this project. These are some examples of good arm twigs (from left to right, top to bottom): Wild grape, two types of oak, azalea, locust, and dogwood.

Clean your hands thoroughly before using white clay. Take a 2 ounce block of Sculpey White and cut it into four equal 1/2 ounce blocks. Each 1/2 ounce block will make one snowman.

Take one of these blocks and pinch off a small amount to make two small balls about the size of two large green peas. Save these for later.

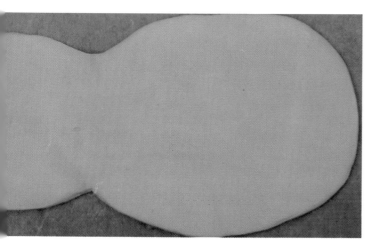

Flatten the rest of the quarter block and shape it into the snowman body or roll out the clay, lay the cut out pattern on top, and cut out the body with a knife.

Position one of the twig arms onto the back of the body. Slightly flatten one of the white balls and press it over the end of the twig to hold firmly in place. Do the same for the other twig and place the snowman right-side up on a glass baking sheet.

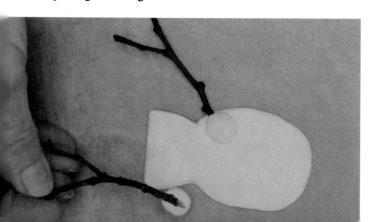

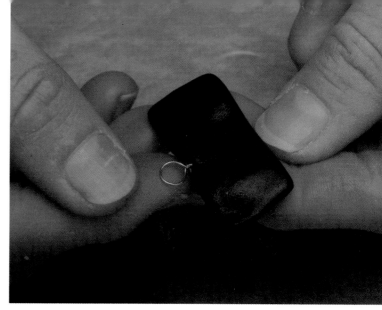

Knead a small piece of Cernit Black and shape into the hat pattern. Insert the wire hanging loop in the center of the top of the hat.

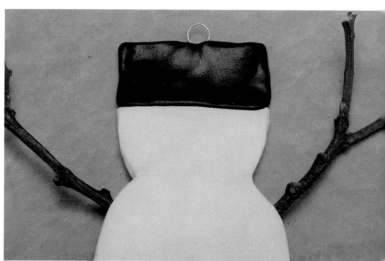

Press the hat firmly onto the top of the snowman, overlapping the head slightly.

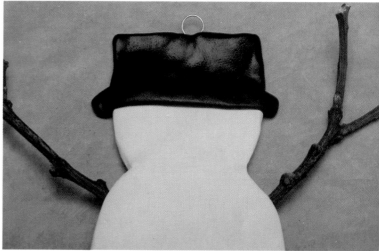

Roll a long, thin strip of Cernit Black slightly longer than the hat for the hat brim. Press in place.

17

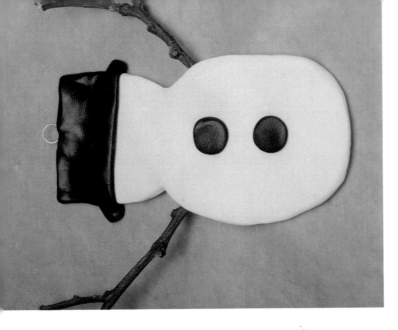

Roll two small balls of black for the buttons. Flatten and press in place.

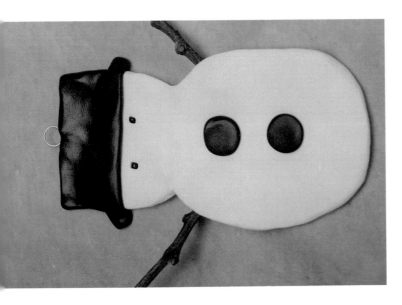

Pick up two black seed beads with a hat pin. Press in place for eyes.

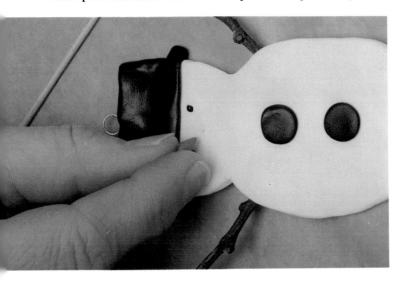

Make a small teardrop shaped piece out of Sculpey Rose for the nose. Make a hole in the center of the face with a toothpick and insert the nose, point first. Press down firmly.

Make a long, thin roll of Cernit Red for the mouth. Lay in position and press down firmly.

Roll two small balls of Sculpey Pink Pearl for the cheeks. Press onto ends of mouth ... firmly.

Press in a red seed bead on the hat brim.

Make holly leaves of Pro Mat Green Pearl as in the first project, pressing one on each side of the red seed bead. Make leaf veins with a hat pin.

Bake at 265 degrees for 30 minutes. You will need a 6" length of 3/8" wide plaid ribbon for the scarf. I buy a 7/16" wide ribbon, cut a 6" length, and then cut this length-wise into four equal strips.

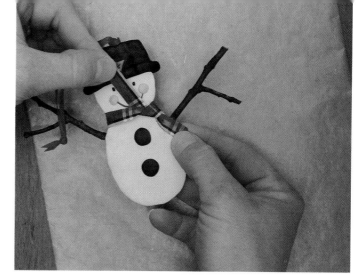

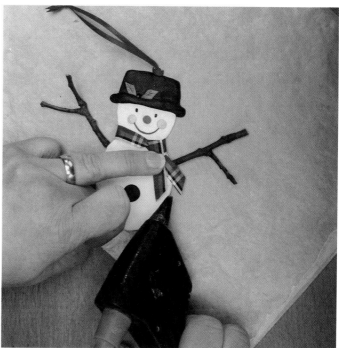

When the snowman has baked and cooled, carefully pop him off the baking sheet and check for loose twigs. If the twigs are loose, add a drop of glue to the holes and reinsert the twigs. Now, heat up a glue gun, wrap the scarf around the snowman's neck as shown, and glue the scarf in place with hot glue. The idea is to have both loose ends of the scarf running down the snowman's side.

Make and attach the hanging cord.

PENGUIN

Penguin. The materials you will need: Sculpey White, Sculpey Black, Sculpey Yellow, Scupley Pink Pearl, Pro Mat Orange, Pro Mat Blue Pearl, Pro Mat Red Pearl, pre-baked candy cane, wire hanging loop, hanging ribbon, ribbon for scarf, and hot glue.

For the penguin, cut a 2 ounce block of Sculpey White into four equal blocks as in the snowman pattern. Cut one of these quarter blocks in half as shown, and save one half for later.

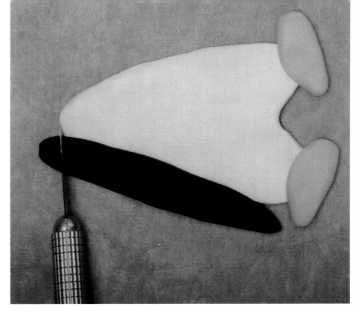

Roll a piece of Sculpey Black, flatten slightly, and shape into the penguin's back. Press in place and cut off the excess at top.

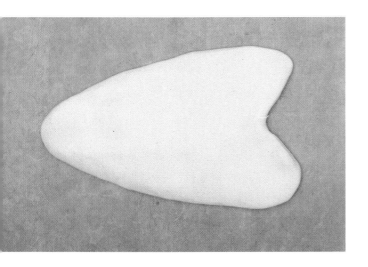

Shape the other half into the body of the penguin. Place the body on your glass baking sheet.

Make a round ball of black and flatten to form the head. Press into place on top of the body.

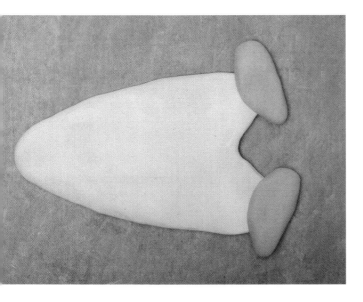

Make two flat ovals of Sculpey Yellow for feet. Press in place.

While you're using the black clay, shape two flippers. Set them aside.

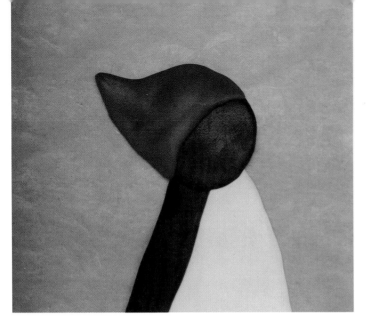

Knead a small piece of Pro Mat Blue Pearl, shape it into a hat, and press onto the head.

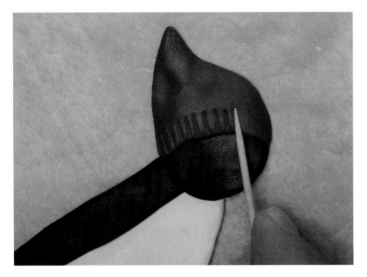

Make a knit edge along the cap with a toothpick.

Insert the hanging loop into the hat.

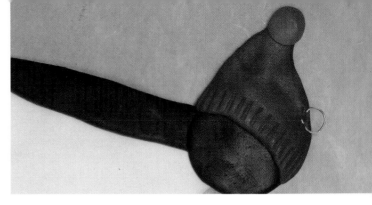

Make a small ball of Pro Mat Red Pearl and press onto the end of the hat.

Knead a small amount of Pro Mat Orange and shape into a small, flat diamond shape.

Fold the diamond shape to form the penguin's beak.

Carefully press the beak onto the head with your fingertips and a toothpick.

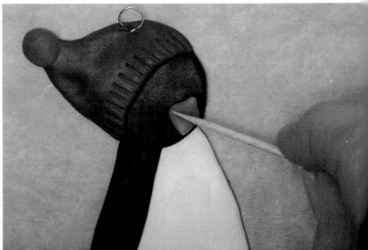

Roll two small, white ovals for eyes and press in place.

Make two black dots and press in place to create pupils.

Press tiny pieces of white onto the black pupils for "shine."

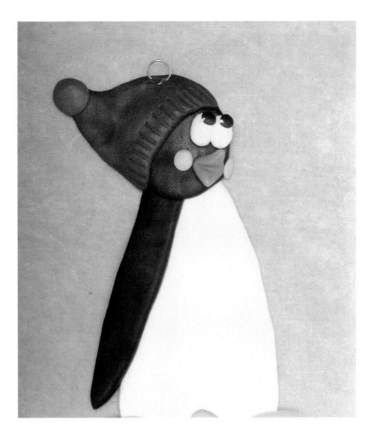

Make two small balls of Sculpey Pink Pearl for cheeks. Press in place.

Attach the flippers now.

Press in pre-baked candy cane.

Bend the two flippers into place, one onto the candy cane.

Bake at 265 degrees for 30 minutes. When baked and cooled, wrap and glue the scarf in place as detailed in the last project. Attach the hanging ribbon.

GINGERBREAD MAN

Gingerbread man. Materials: Sculpey Bronze, Sculpey Rose, Pro Mat Red Pearl, Sculpey Pink Pearl, Pro Mat Green Pearl, two black seed beads, one red seed bead, two green seed beads, a hanging loop, and ribbon for hanging.

Create and insert the hanging loop into the top of the head.

For the gingerbread man, roll out Sculpey Bronze on your pasta machine at setting 1 (about 2 mm. thick). Cut out the gingerbread man's body with the pattern.

Press in two black seed beads for eyes.

Press two small balls of Sculpey Pink Pearl at the ends of the mouth for cheeks.

Make a teardrop shaped nose out of Sculpey Rose. Make a hole in the face with a toothpick and press in the nose (point side down).

Make a long, thin line of Pro Mat Red Pearl for the mouth and press in place.

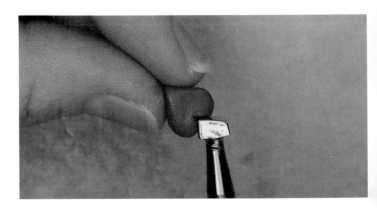

Make a heart by rolling a small ball of Pro Mat Red Pearl, flattening it and shaping one end into a point. Press an indentation into the rounded side with a toothpick, a fingernail, or a square-headed tool to make a heart shape.

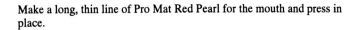

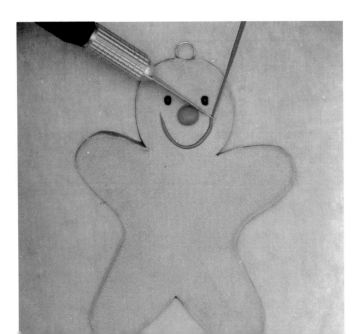

Press the heart onto the body as shown.

Slightly curl one hand if you want your gingerbread man to wave.

Pick up a red seed bead with a hat pin and press into the center of the neck. Now pick up two green seed beads and press them into the body as buttons.

Make two green leaves, as in previous projects, and place one on each side of the red seed bead. Make leaf veins with a hat pin.

Bake at 265 degrees for 34 minutes. When baked and cooled, attach a hanging ribbon.

GIFT BEARING POLAR BEAR

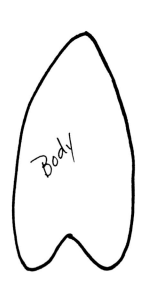

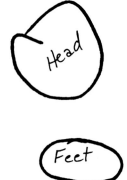

Gift Bearing Polar Bear. Materials: Sculpey White, Sculpey Black, Pro Mat Red Pearl, Green Pearl, Gold Pearl, and Blue Pearl, two black seed beads, wire hanging loop, ribbon for hanging, and a pre-baked Christmas package.

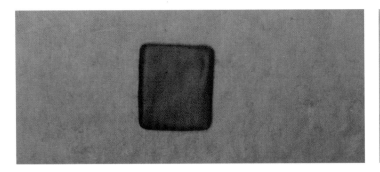

To make the Christmas Package, knead a small amount of Pro Mat Red Pearl and shape into the gift pattern.

Create a long, thin roll of Pro Mat Green Pearl, flatten, and cut into ribbon pieces for the gift.

Press ribbon onto the gift as shown.

Make two small triangles of Pro Mat Green Pearl for bows. Attach at the top of the gift by pressing firmly.

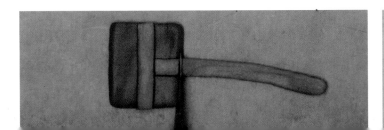

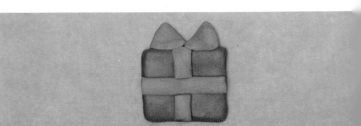

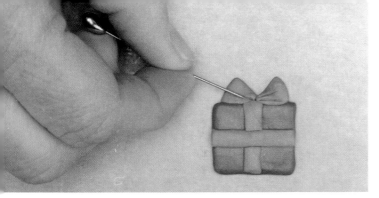

Make indentations in the bows with a hat pin or toothpick.

Add a green dot in the center for the knot in the bow. Bake at 265 degrees for 20 minutes. Allow to cool.

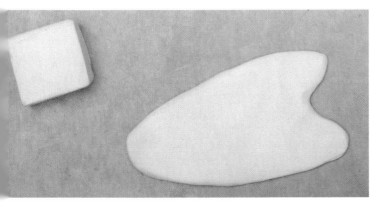

Take a 1/4 block (1/2 ounce) of Sculpey White. This should make one bear. Cut the block in half and shape 1/2 into the bear's body.

With part of the other half, shape the head. Pinch up a portion for the muzzle.

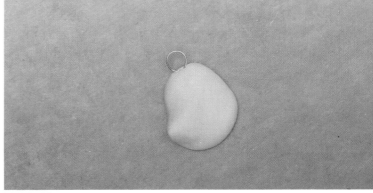

Insert the hanging loop.

Roll two small ovals out of Sculpey White for the ears and press onto the head.

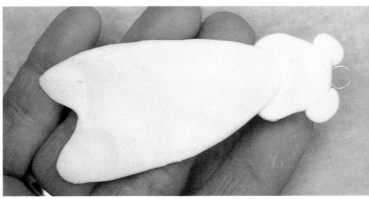

Carefully, but firmly, attach the head to the body.

Press in two black seed beads for eyes.

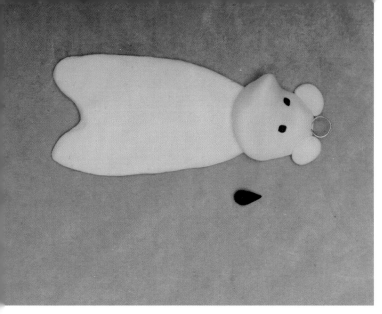

Roll a small black teardrop shape for the bear's nose.

Make a smile with the tip of a toothpick.

Make a hole in the tip of the muzzle with a toothpick and insert the nose with the pointed end down. Press in without flattening the muzzle too much.

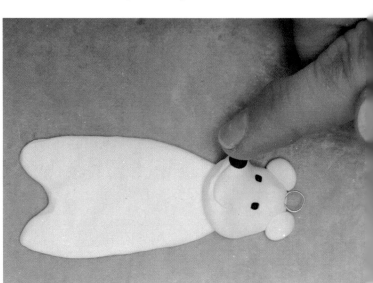

At this point check to see if your bear looks too mouse-like. If he does, press in the muzzle a bit more and make smaller ears.

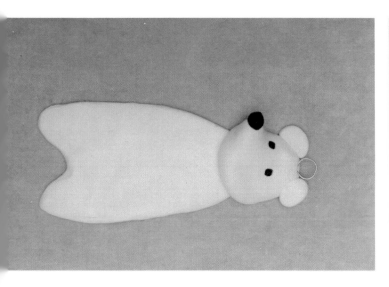

Like so.

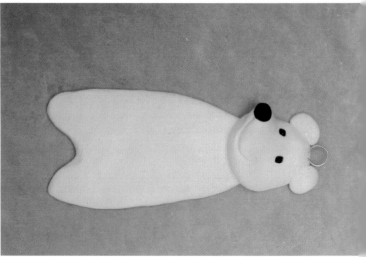

Like so.

Shape the Sculpey White into the shape of the foot pattern. Make two feet and attach them to the legs.

Press pre-baked gift onto the center of the body and press the paws onto the sides of the gift.

Roll out two rolls of Sculpey White. Round one end and make the other end come to a rounded point. The rounded point is the shoulder attachment.

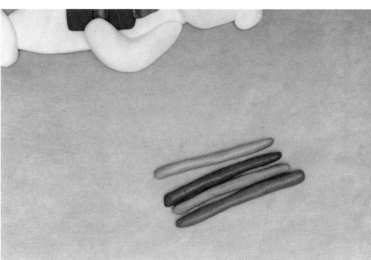

For the scarf, make thin rolls of Pro Mat Red Pearl, Green Pearl, Blue Pearl, and Gold Pearl.

Bend the arms in the center and press onto the body at the shoulders.

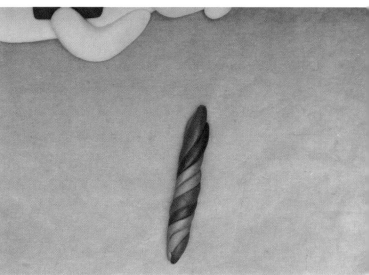

Twist the strands together to form one roll.

31

Continue rolling the combined strands, making the roll thinner and longer. Then flatten it into the scarf shape.

Cut off a small piece and press onto the bear's neck.

Cut off a piece for the rest of the scarf and press onto the bear's neck.

Fringe the ends with a knife tip.

The finished bear. Bake at 265 degrees for 30 minutes. When cooled, attach a hanging ribbon.

Like so.

RIBBON SANTA

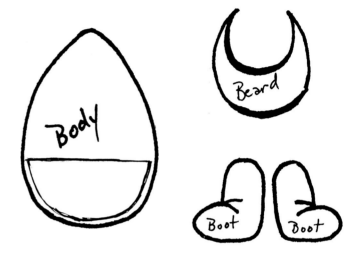

Ribbon Santa Ornament. Materials: Super Sculpey, Cernit Black, Sculpey White, Sculpey Pink Pearl, Sculpey Rose, red and green seed beads, two black seed beads, a wire hanging loop, 1/8" wide ribbon for arms, legs, and for hanging.

The first thing to do is make the Santa face. To make the face, roll a small ball of Super Sculpey and flatten it slightly until it is roughly the size of a nickel.

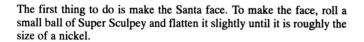

Press in two black seed beads for eyes. Use a hat pin to carve in the eye and forehead lines. This makes wider and deeper lines than a knife could. Knife lines tend to close up and become hard to see.

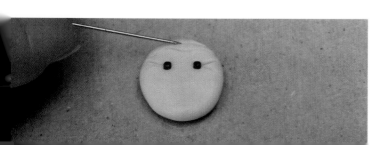

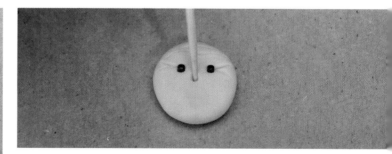

Take a tooth pick and make a hole for the nose to secure it properly.

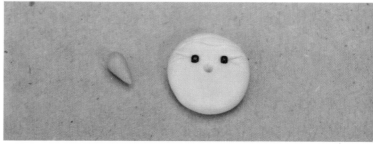

The nose is shaped like this out of Sculpey Rose.

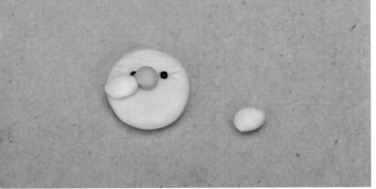 

Insert the nose and make two small balls of Sculpey Pink Pearl for the cheeks. Press them into place alongside of the nose.

For the mustache, roll two plump teardrop shapes from Sculpey white.

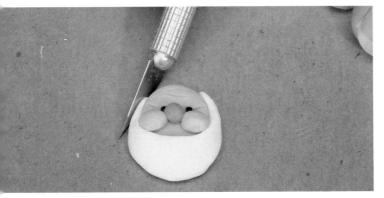

I take white clay and shape the beard by hand and check it against the pattern for size. You may also roll the clay out, lay the pattern over the clay, and cut out around the pattern with a knife. Press the beard into place with an X-acto knife and press it down firmly. Note: when working with white, make sure your hands are perfectly clean.

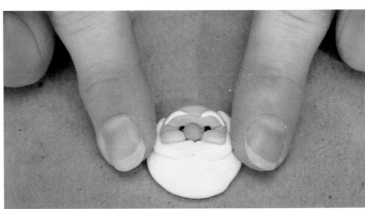

Press the mustache into place and curve up the ends into the beard to give the impression that Santa is smiling. The face is complete. Now bake it at 265 degrees for 30 minutes.

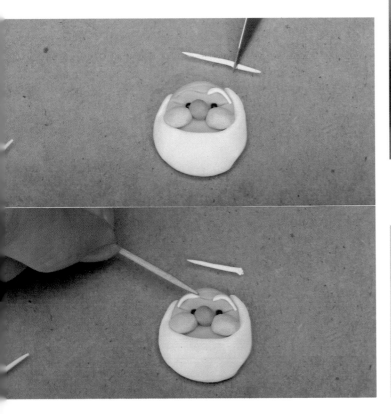

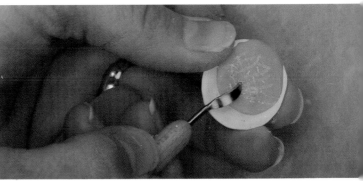

When cool, roughen up the back surface with a knife or sandpaper to make it adhere more tightly to the clay.

Create a thin roll of clay and cut off two thin pieces for the eyebrows with the X-acto knife. Press firmly into place.

Make a small ball of Pro Mat Red Pearl and flatten until it is slightly smaller than the back of the head.

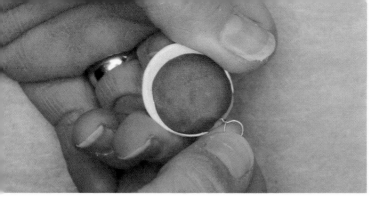

Press this flattened red ball onto the back of Santa's head. Insert the wire hanging loop into this flattened ball at the top of the head.

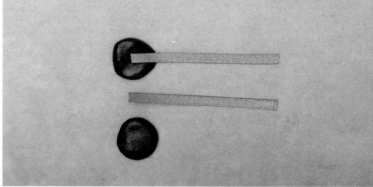

Flatten two small balls of Cernit Black for the hands. Lay about 1/4" of ribbon onto each hand.

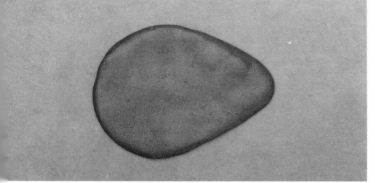

Knead more Pro Mat Red Pearl and form it into the shape of the body pattern.

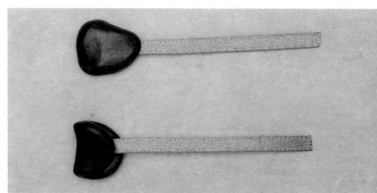

Fold the clay over the ribbon and shape into hands as shown.

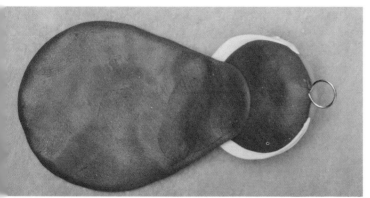

Attach the head to the body, press the head very firmly into place.

Cut two 2" long strips of 1/8" wide ribbon for the arms. Cut two 1 1/2" long strips for the legs.

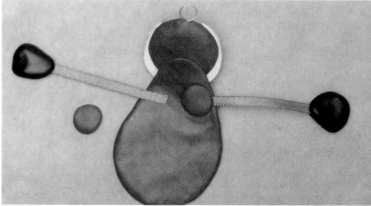

Carefully lay each ribbon arm onto Santa's back and press two flattened balls of Pro Mat Red Pearl over the ribbon ends to secure them.

Turn Santa over and lay him on a glass baking sheet. Make finger indentations in each hand with a toothpick.

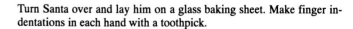

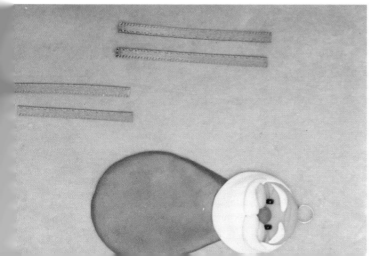

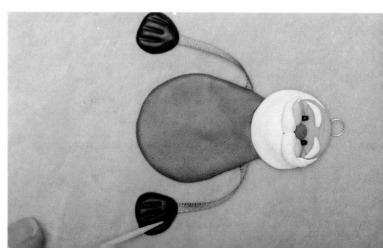

For the legs, lay one end of each ribbon onto a kneaded piece of Cernit Black.

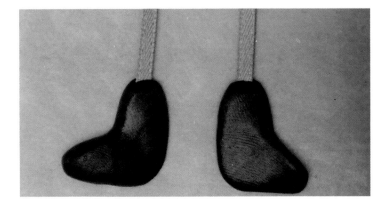

Fold the clay over the ribbon end and shape the clay into a boot.

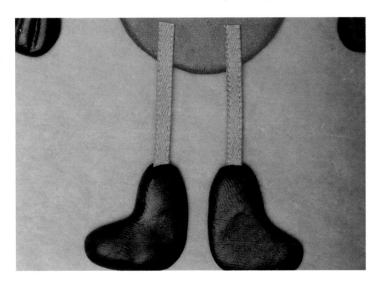

Align the boots with the ribbon ends laying on top of the bottom edge of Santa's body.

Shape a piece of Pro Mat Red Pearl into a crescent shape.

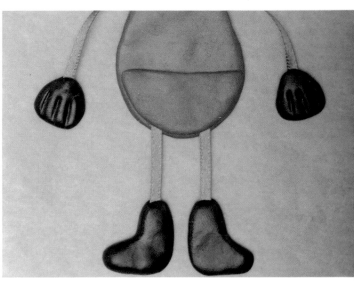

Lay this piece over the ribbon ends and press firmly.

Make creases in the boots with a toothpick.

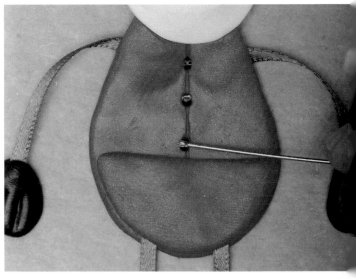

Make a line on the front of the body and press in three green seed beads for buttons.

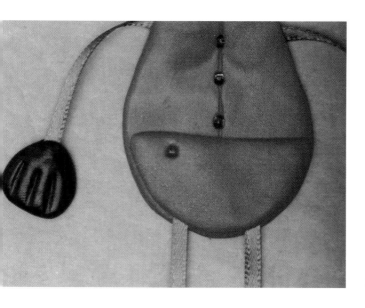

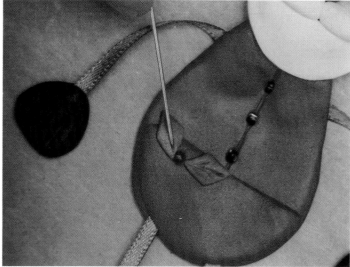

Press in one red seed bead on top of the front flap of the crescent that covers the ribbon legs.

Make leaves out of Pro Mat Green Pearl. Press one on either side of the seed bead and make leaf veins with a hat pin.

Bake at 265 degrees for 30 minutes and, when cool, attach a hanging ribbon.

CHRISTMAS PIG

Christmas Pig. Materials: Super Sculpey, Sculpey Pink Pearl, Pro Mat Red Pearl, Blue Pearl, and Green Pearl, one red seed bead, two black seed beads, a wire hanging loop, a pre-baked candy cane, and ribbon for hanging.

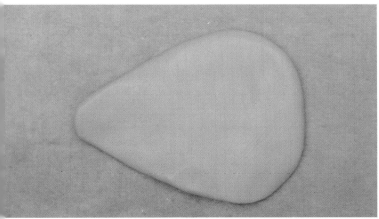

For the Christmas Pig, knead Super Sculpey well and shape into the body pattern.

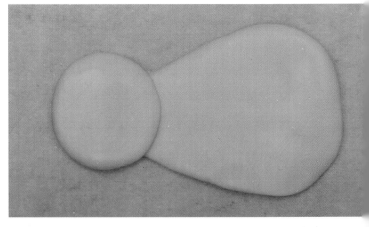

Shape a piece of Super Sculpey for the head and press firmly on top of the body.

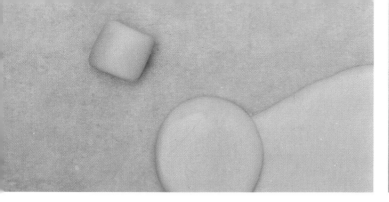

Make a Super Sculpey cylinder for the snout.

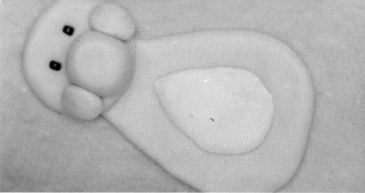

Make a flat, teardrop shape of Sculpey Pink Pearl for the tummy. Press into place.

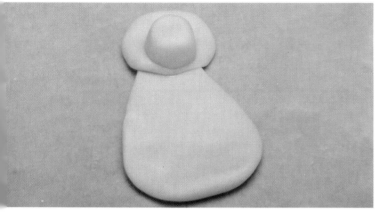

Press carefully onto the face.

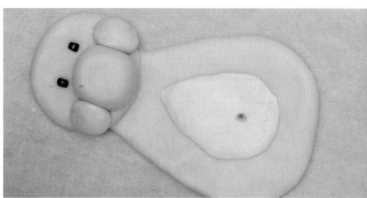

Make a belly button with the tip of a toothpick.

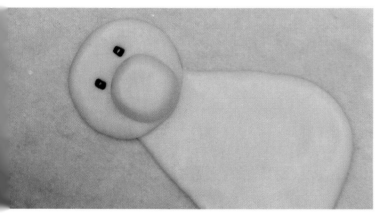

Press in two black seed beads for eyes.

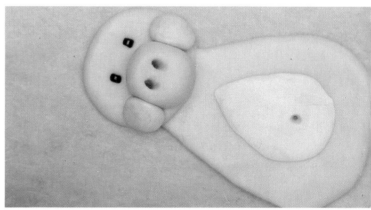

Make two nostril ovals in the snout with a toothpick.

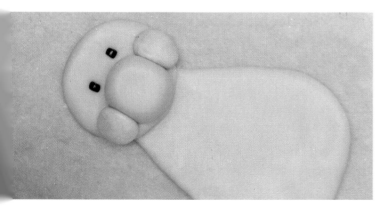

Make two small balls of Sculpey Pink Pearl for the cheeks. Press one on each side of the snout.

Also make a few wrinkles along the top of the nose with a toothpick.

Knead Pro Mat Red Pearl and shape it into a tall, pointed hat. Press onto the top of the pigs head.

Insert the hanging loop into the top of the hat.

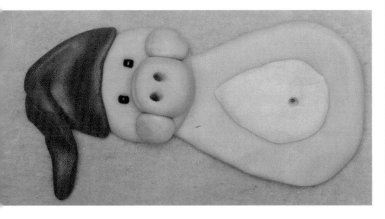

Fold the top of the hat down so that it flops over a bit.

Make two flattened diamond shapes out of Super Sculpey for the ears.

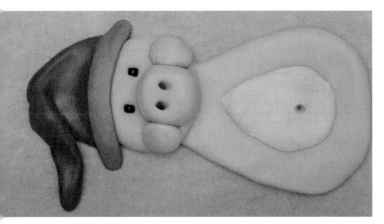

Add a thin, flattened roll of Pro Mat Green Pearl for the brim.

Attach firmly with your fingertips or a toothpick.

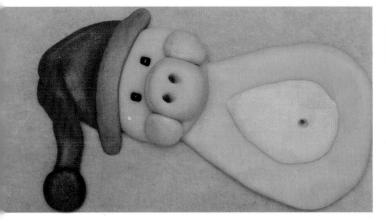

Add a small ball of Pro Mat Blue Pearl for the tip of the hat.

Fold the ears down and out.

Using Super Sculpey, shape two legs and press firmly onto the lower body.

Press a pre-baked candy cane onto the body.

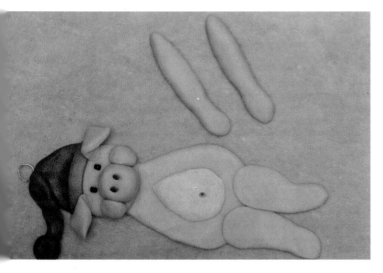

Shape two arms out of Super Sculpey.

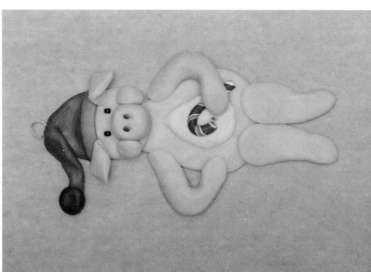

Press one of the pig's "hands" onto the candy cane and the other hand onto the tummy or the hips.

Bend the arms slightly and attach them at the shoulders.

Make hoof indentations in the feet and hands with a toothpick.

Make wrinkles at the elbows with a toothpick. Press in a red seed bead on the pig's neck.

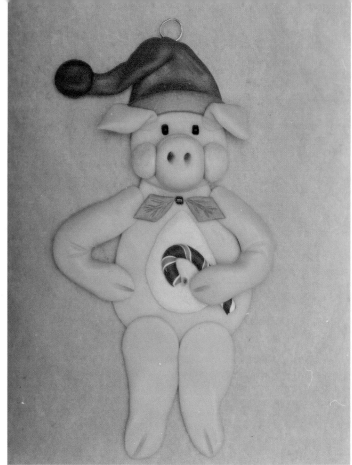

Make two leaves out of Pro Mat Green Pearl. Press one on each side of the seed bead. Make leaf veins with a hat pin. Bake the finished pig at 265 degrees for 34 minutes.

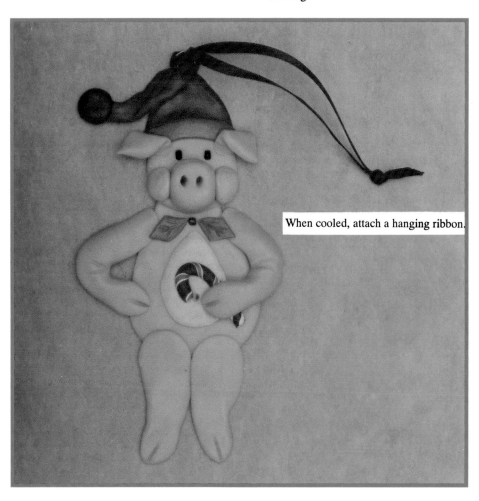

When cooled, attach a hanging ribbon.

BUNNY ANGEL

Bunny Angel Ornament. Materials: Cernit Glamour White, Sculpey White, Sculpey Yellow, Sculpey Rose, Sculpey Pink Pearl, Pro Mat Green Pearl, black seed bead, 20 gauge wire for a wand, a wire hanging loop, hanging ribbon, one red seed bead, and a wire candy cane.

The wire candy cane was cut from a larger cane purchased at a craft shop. Each large cane may be cut into three small candy canes which are the perfect size for this project. Curve the candy canes with round-nose pliers.

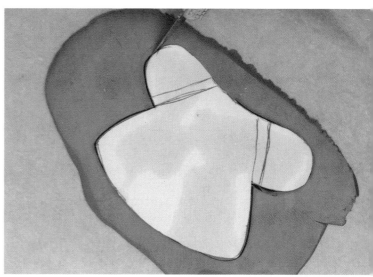

Roll out the Sculpey Rose on pasta machine setting 2 (a little less than 2 mm. thick). Cut out the dress pattern.

Wash your hands thoroughly (the pink will ruin your white), knead the Cernit Glamour White, and shape it into the head and both ears.

Insert a hanging loop into the back ear and press the back ear into place behind the front ear. Set the head aside.

While you are working with the Glamour White, go ahead and shape the feet and hands. Set them aside.

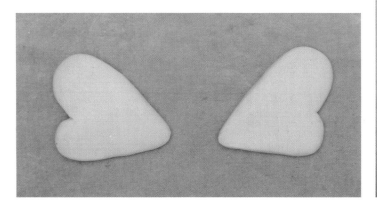

Shape or cut out two wings of Sculpey White.

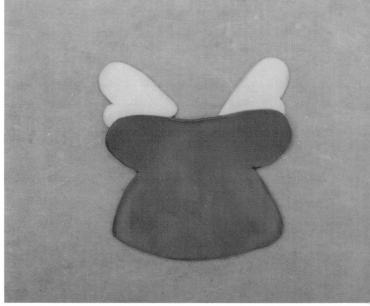

Place the wings on the baking sheet, gently place the dress over the edges of the wings, and press in place.

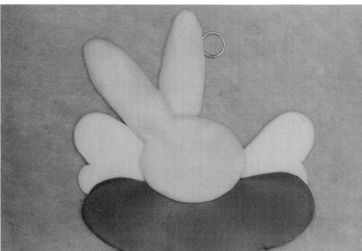

Position head and ears in place. Press firmly over both the dress and wings.

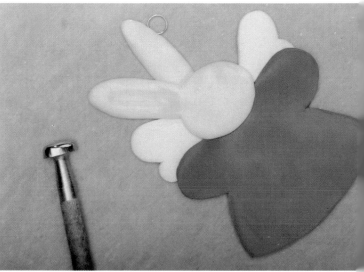

Make an indentation in the front ear with a small round-headed tool.

Lay a thin strip of Sculpey Pink Pearl over the ear indentation and press in again with the small round-headed tool.

Press in a black seed bead for the eye. Use a small dot of Sculpey Pink Pearl for the nose.

Place hands under the sleeves of the dress and press into place.

Place the feet beneath the hem of the dress.

Make indentations in the wings and feet with a toothpick.

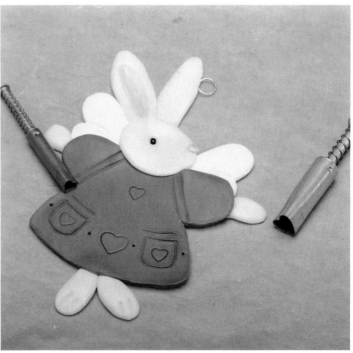

Make designs on the dress with a toothpick and heart stamps as shown on the pattern.

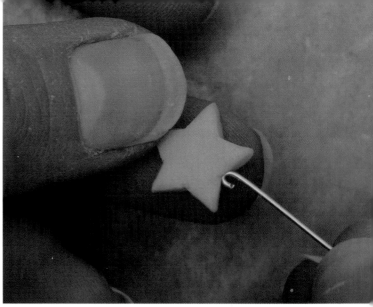

Slide the curved tip of the wire carefully into the star.

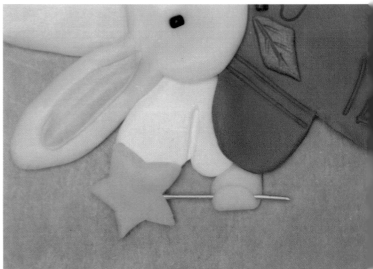

Press in one red seed bead on the neck. Make leaves of Pro Mat Green Pearl and place one on each side of the seed bead. Incise the leaf veins with a hat pin.

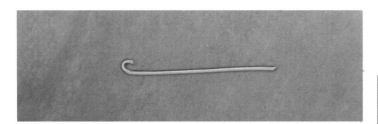

Carefully lay the wand on the angel's right hand, allowing some of the star to rest on the wing. Press down and fold the hand over the wand handle. (Note: if the star loses its shape in this step, remake it and pre-bake it attached to the wire wand.)

Cut a 1 1/8" piece of 20 gauge wire. Bend down the tip as shown with needle-nose pliers. This will keep the wire from slipping out of the clay.

Cut out a star from a flattened piece of Sculpey Yellow.

Lay the wire candy cane in the center of the angel's left hand. Fold the hand over to secure.

Make finger indentations on the hands with a toothpick.

Bake at 265 degrees for 30 minutes. When cool, attach a hanging ribbon.

Puppy In A Stocking

Puppy in a Stocking. Materials: Cernit Red, Super Sculpey, Sculpey White, Black, Yellow, Rose, and Green Brilliant, two black seed beads, a wire hanging loop, and a ribbon for hanging.

under stocking

Head

Ears & Paws

(make 4)

stocking

Hat

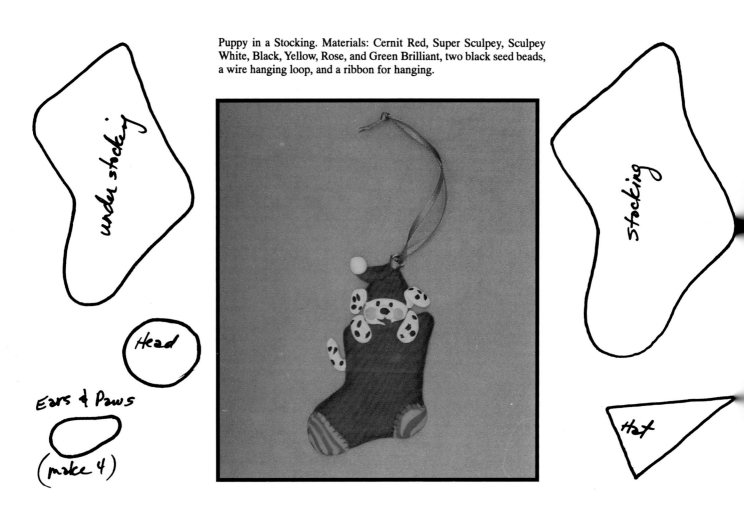

Begin by shaping the under-stocking out of Super Sculpey.

Knead the Cernit Red and shape it by hand into the red stocking or roll the Cernit Red out and cut it out using the pattern.

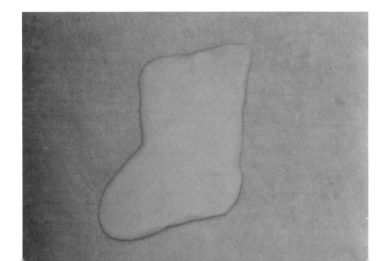

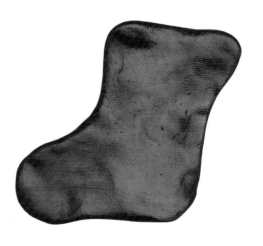

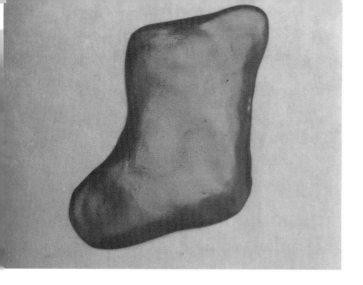

Lay the red stocking down lightly over the under-stocking. Press down from the middle out to help prevent air bubbles. If you do get air bubbles, pierce them with a knife tip and press out the air.

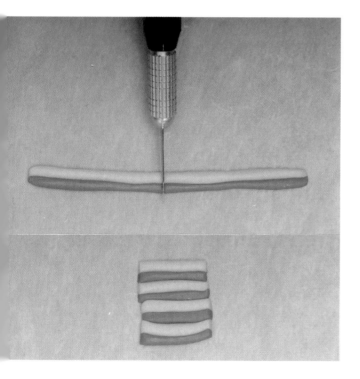

Make two long thin rolls of clay, one Sculpey Green Brilliant, the other Sculpey Yellow. Lay side-by-side. Cut in half, lay these two parts side-by-side, and repeat one more time.

Press these together to form a smooth, solid sheet of stripes.

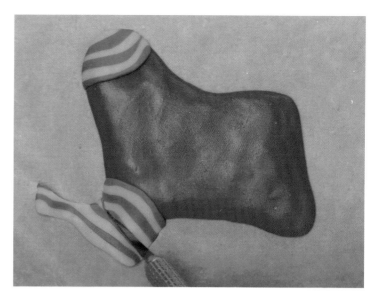

Cut a toe and heel piece and place them on the stocking. Curve down over the sides of the toe and the heel.

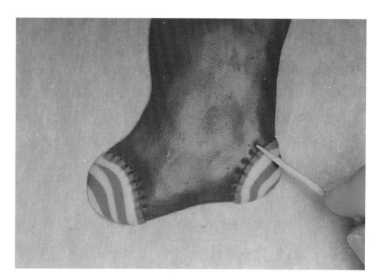

Make stitch marks with a toothpick.

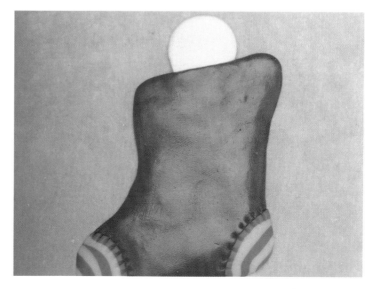

Make a small circle of white clay for the head. Press in just under the stocking edge.

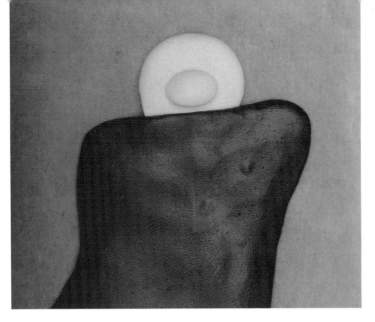

Make a small oval of white for the muzzle and press into place.

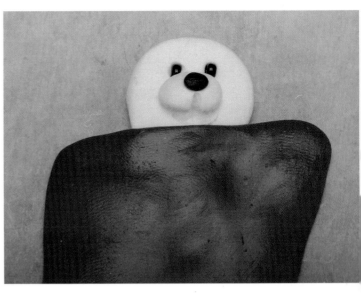

Divide the underside of the muzzle in half with a toothpick and gently open up the clay below the muzzle to form a smiling mouth.

Press in two black seed beads for eyes.

Color the inside of the mouth with a tiny bit of Sculpey Rose. Make a tiny tongue to hang out the front. Place the tongue with the tip of a toothpick.

Add a small, black oval for the nose.

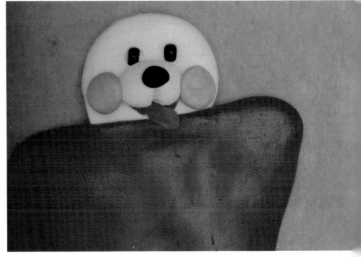

Add two small balls of Sculpey Pink Pearl for puppy cheeks.

Make a tall hat out of Cernit Red, press it onto the top of the head, and bend the top down so that the hat flops over.

Press in the hanging loop. Press on a small ball of Sculpey White for the hat as well.

Shape paws and a tail out of Sculpey White and attach as shown.

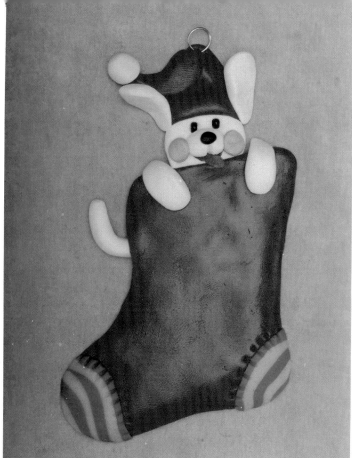

Shape ears and attach to the sides of the head.

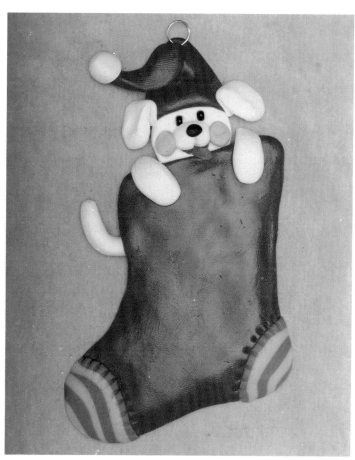

Bend the ears over to look "puppy-ish."

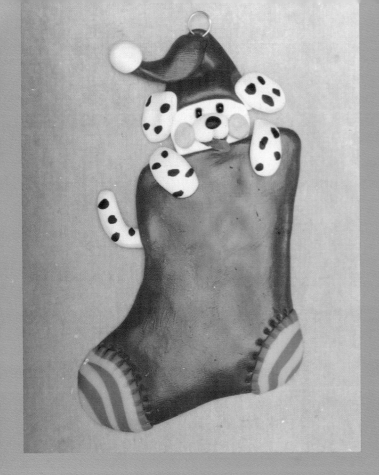 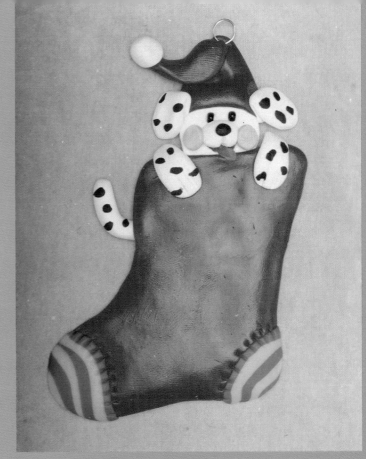

Pinch off small dots of Sculpey Black. Press onto the puppy's ears, tail, and paws.

Press in paw indentations with a toothpick.

Bake at 265 degrees for 30 minutes. When cooled, attach the hanging ribbon.

THE GALLERY

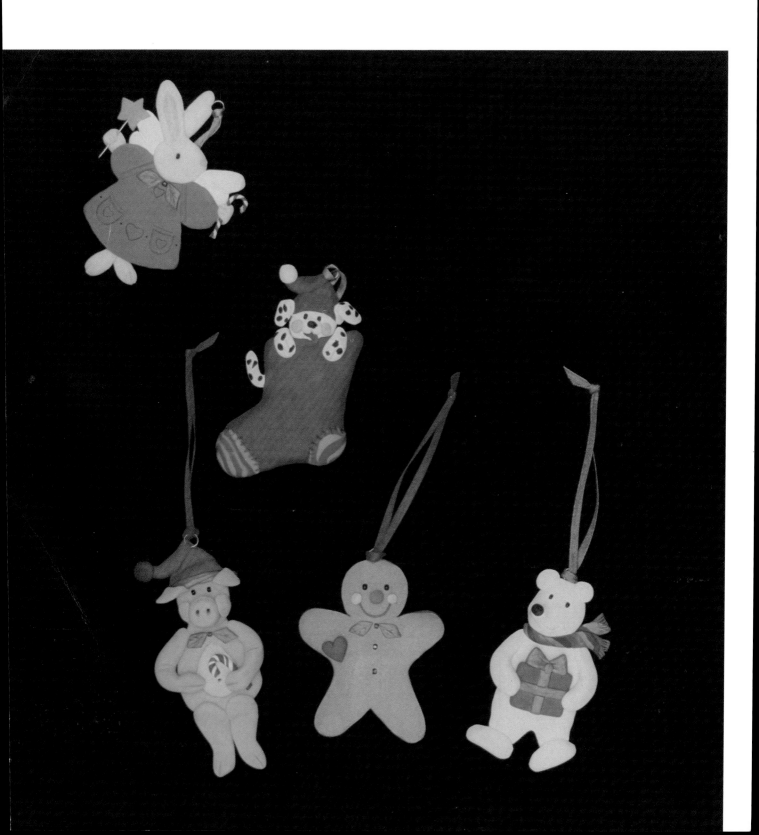

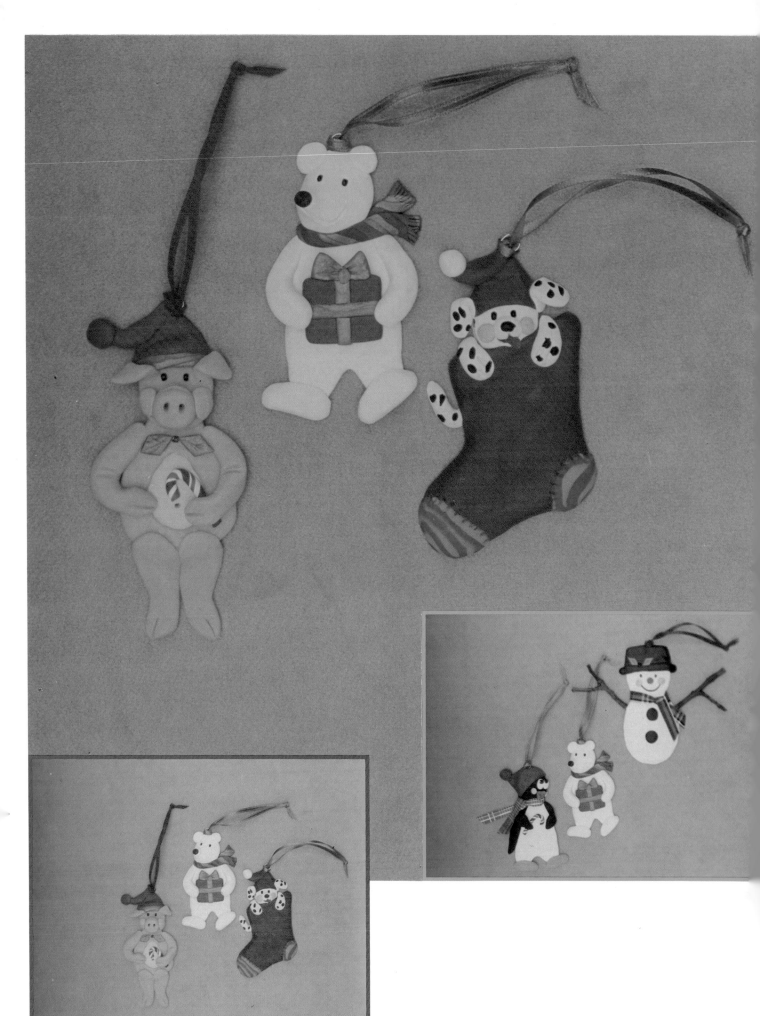

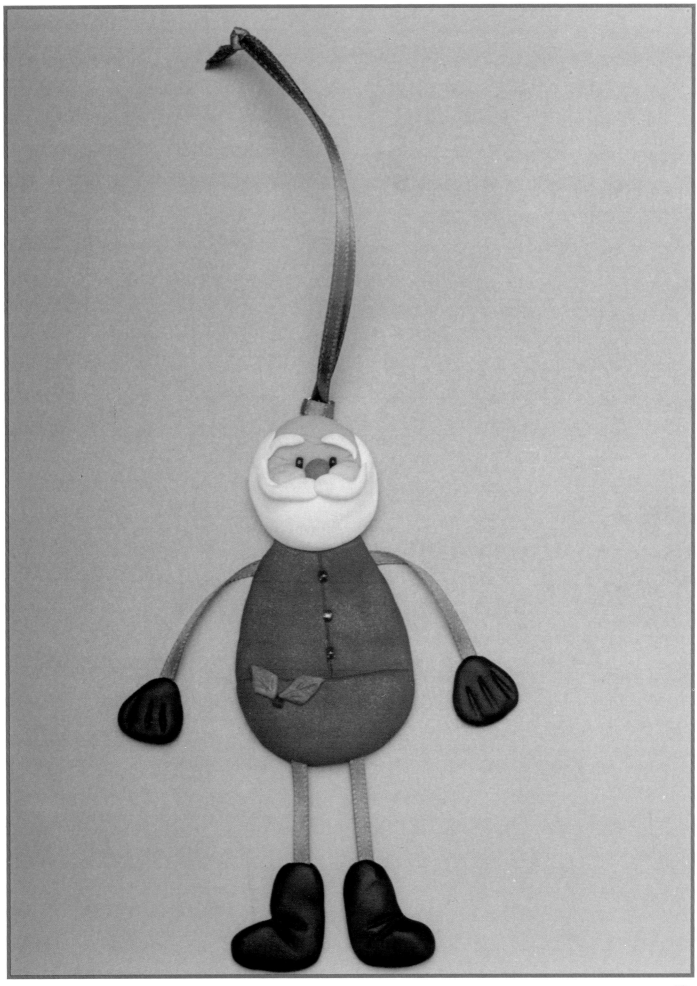

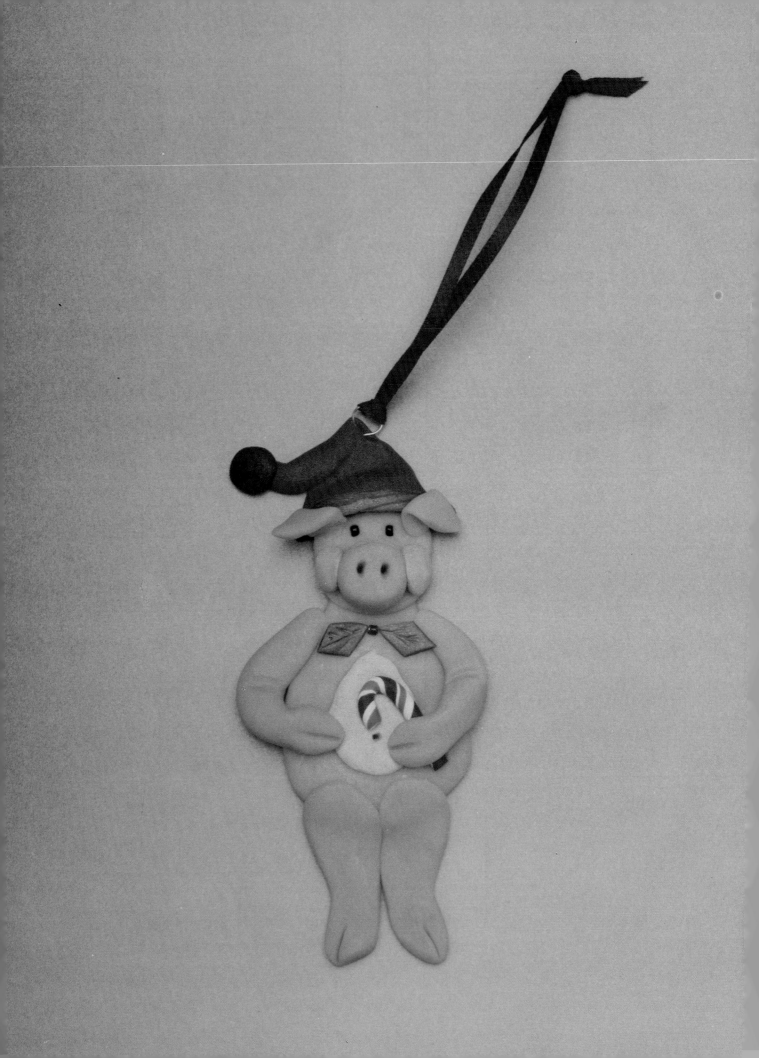

Merry Christmas